Rookie
Read-About Science®

W9-CDM-897

They Could Still Be Mountains WITHDRAWN

By Allan Fowler

Consultants

Linda Cornwell, Learning Resource Consultant,
Indiana Department of Education

Fay Robinson, Child Development Specialist

Lynne Kepler, Educational Consultant

Children's Press®
A Division of Grolier Publishing
New York   London   Hong Kong   Sydney
Danbury, Connecticut

Project Editor: Downing Publishing Services
Designer: Herman Adler Design Group
Photo Researcher: Caroline Anderson

Library of Congress Cataloging-in-Publication Data

Fowler, Allan.
    They could still be mountains / by Allan Fowler.
      p. cm. – (Rookie read-about science)
    Includes index.
    Summary: Discusses different kinds of mountains, old and new,
how they were formed, and how they can change over time.
    ISBN 0-516-20320-7 (lib.bdg.)   0-516-26159-2 (pbk.)
    1. Mountains—Juvenile literature. [l. Mountains.] I. Title. II. Series
GB512.F69   1997   96-28292
551.4'32–dc20   CIP
                                           AC

You can see why these
mountains are called the
Rocky Mountains. They have
steep sides of bare, jagged
rock, rising to sharp peaks.

Their lower slopes
might be covered by
thick forests, where
bears and deer roam.

Higher up the slopes,
it's too cold for trees
to grow. You find just
mosses and shrubs.

mountain goat

You might also see
sure-footed animals,
such as bighorn sheep
and mountain goats,
leaping from crag to crag.

Still higher, nothing grows. At the very top, it's so cold that the snow and ice never melt away, even in summer.

The Rocky Mountains cover
a good part of the western
United States and Canada.

Not all mountains look like the Rockies. They could be lower . . . with rounded tops and sloping sides . . . green with trees all the way up to their tops . . . and they could still be mountains.

The Appalachian
Mountains are like that.
They stretch from Quebec
in Canada as far south as
the state of Alabama.

The Appalachians look very different from the Rockies because they are much older.

Once they were high, rugged peaks like the Rockies. But over a long, long time, the Appalachians were worn down by water, ice, and wind — until they became the way they are today.

A group of mountains, such as the Rockies or Appalachians, is called a range. The world's highest mountain range is the Himalayas in Asia.

The top of Mount Everest, one of the Himalayas, is the highest place in the world.

The low land between
mountains is called
a valley. Rivers often
run through valleys.

Glaciers — thick sheets of ice — move slowly down from some mountains.

Mountains could lie
completely under
the sea — and still
be mountains.

An island could be the
top of a mountain rising
from the sea bottom.

Certain mountains are
known as volcanoes.
From time to time,
a volcano erupts.

That is, lava pours
out of its crater, a big
hole at its top. The lava
runs down the sides of
the volcano.

Lava is hot liquid rock.
It comes from deep inside
the earth, where rock is
melted by the great heat.

Your parents might remember when a volcano, Mount St. Helens, erupted in the United States.

But don't worry — most
mountains aren't volcanoes.

Many families visit
mountains on their
vacations. Skiing down
the slopes of a mountain
is a popular winter sport.

Another sport — mountain climbing — takes lots of skill and courage.

Some people hike on
mountain trails.

You can hike all the way
from Maine to Georgia
(or from Georgia to
Maine) along the
Appalachian Trail —
more than 2,000 miles.

Now that's quite a walk!

But even if you don't ski, climb, or hike, you can simply enjoy the beautiful mountain scenery.

Which would you rather look at — bare, rocky peaks, or green, rounded hills?

Words You Know

Appalachian Mountains

Himalayas

Rocky Mountains

mountain

valley

river

glacier

volcano

lava

crater

Index

Alabama, 10
animals, 5, 6
Appalachian Trail, 27
Appalachian Mountains
  (Appalachians), 10, 13,
  14, 30
bears, 5
bighorn sheep, 6
Canada, 8, 10
crag, 6
crater, 20, 31
deer, 5
earth, 21
eruption, of volcanoes, 20
forests, 5
Georgia, 27
glaciers, 17, 31
heat, 21
hiking, 27, 28
hills, 28

Himalayas, 14, 15, 30
ice, 7, 13, 17
island, 18
lava, 20, 31
Maine, 27
mosses, 5
Mount St. Helens, 22
Mount Everest, 15
mountain climbing, 25, 28
mountain goats, 6
mountain range, 14
mountains
  new, with bare, jagged
  steep peaks, 3, 13, 28
  old, with rounded tops
  and sloping sides, 3,
  13, 28
mountain trails, 27
peaks, 3, 13
Quebec, 10
rivers, 16, 31

rock
  bare, jagged, 3
  hot, liquid, 21
Rocky Mountains
  (Rockies), 3, 8, 9, 13,
  14, 30
scenery, 28
sea, 18
shrubs, 5
skiing, 24, 28
slopes, 5, 9, 24
snow, 7
summer, 7
trees, 5, 9
United States, 8, 22
vacations, 24
valleys, 16, 31
volcanoes, 20, 22, 23, 31
water, 13
wind, 13
winter sports, 24

About the Author

Allan Fowler is a free-lance writer with a background in advertising.
Born in New York, he lives in Chicago now and enjoys traveling.

Photo Credits

Valan Photos — ©Aubrey Diem, cover, 16, 31 (top left); ©J. R. Page, 3, 4, 17,
30 (bottom left), 31 (middle left); ©Esther Schmidt, 6, 31 (top right); ©Halle
Flygare, 7, 23; ©Jean Sloman, 8; ©Phillip Norton, 9, 12; ©François Morneau,
11, 30 (top left); ©B. Templeman, 14, 15, 25, 30 (top right); S. J. Krasemann,
19, 31 (bottom right); ©Kennon Cooke, 24; Jean-Marie Jro, 30 (bottom right)
Comstock — ©H. Kinne, 21, 31 (bottom left)
United States Geological Survey (USGS) — ©R. Hoblitt, 22, 31 (middle right)
Ellis Nature Photography — ©Michael Durham, 26
COVER: Matterhorn, Zermatt, Switzerland